DAVID HALL

MEDIEVAL FIELDS

SHIRE ARCHAEOLOGY

Cover illustration
Medieval ridge and furrow at Naseby, Northamptonshire.

Published by
SHIRE PUBLICATIONS LTD
Cromwell House, Church Street, Princes Risborough,
Aylesbury, Bucks, HP17 9AJ, UK.

Series Editor: James Dyer

ISBN 0 85263 599 0

First published 1982; reprinted 1987.

Set in 12 on 11 point Times roman
and printed in Great Britain by
C. I. Thomas & Sons (Haverfordwest) Ltd,
Press Buildings, Merlins Bridge, Haverfordwest.

Contents

Acknowledgements

I am grateful to the Cambridge University Committee for Aerial Photography for permission to publish fig. 1; to R. T. Rowley for allowing me to use figs. 3 and 26; to the Medieval Village Research Group for permission to publish fig. 32; to B. K. Roberts for pointing out to me the field systems of Middleton (fig. 31); and to P. I. King of the Northamptonshire Record Office for permission to publish figs. 9 and 12.

List of illustrations

Terminology and structure of medieval fields

The medieval landscape was quite unlike that of today. There was not a continuous pattern of hedged fields dotted with trees that occupied the whole parish. In contrast the landscape was open, apart from an occasional royal forest, or a cluster of trees in the paddocks adjacent to a village. Almost all the countryside was arable, the only grass being permanent pastures lying next to brooks and rivers. The arable was subdivided into many tiny plots, which were long in relation to their width. No hedge, fence or ditch demarked these strips, furrows left by the plough being deemed a sufficient boundary.

If it be accepted that the familiar ridge and furrow, often visible in modern fields of permanent pasture (figs. 1, 2), is essentially medieval in origin, then it is a simple matter to identify the physical distribution of these early fields.

Ridge and furrow is often considered to be characteristic of the English Midlands, but it has a much wider distribution, being common in northern English counties, e.g. Staffordshire, Yorkshire and Northumberland. The valleys and lower lying lands of Wales and Scotland also reveal examples, but in East Anglia and Kent none is to be seen. These latter regions did have subdivided open fields, as attested by various maps and surveys, but the strips were not ridged up, so no obvious physical remains are apparent.

The considerable regional variations that exist make it impossible to discuss fully all the local details in this book. Most of the evidence used here applies to the system long identified as characteristic of the English Midlands. Village names mentioned in this book refer to Northamptonshire unless stated otherwise.

Structure of medieval fields

The unit of cultivation was a strip, called a *land,* averaging, in the Midland region, about 7 by 180 metres (8 by 200 yards) or 0.13 hectare ($\frac{1}{3}$ acre). In practice there was considerable variation in size, from 3 to 14 metres (3 to 15 yards) in width and from 14 to 350 metres (15 to 380 yards) in length; however, the average was very often found. In the areas peripheral to the Midlands wide variations exist; thus near Peterborough, on the Welland valley gravel terraces, lands are usually 15 metres (16 yards) wide and average 0.27 hectares ($\frac{2}{3}$ acre) in area.

On the Yorkshire Wolds strips can be as long as 1,000 metres (1,100 yards) and are commonly 9 metres (10 yards) wide (area 0.9 hectares, $2\frac{1}{4}$ acres).

These strips were ploughed in a clockwise manner, more often than anticlockwise, which caused them to be ridged up to about 0.3 metres (1 foot) high in the centre, leaving two flat sides sloping from ridge to furrow. In the north-west of Northamptonshire and in Warwickshire, ridges exist as high as 1 metre (3 feet). Lands were ridged up to assist natural drainage, and for this reason the furrows were aligned down the steepest gradient (unless the terrain sloped very sharply, i.e. steeper than about 1 in 6). Towards the ends of lands there were slight left-handed twists (viewed from the centre), so causing the complete shape to be an elongated mirror image of an S (fig. 3).

The movement of the plough caused transference of a small quantity of soil forwards along the direction of motion (as well as from left to right, forming the ridge). At the end of the land the plough was lifted out for turning and the extra quantity of soil was deposited. This simple soil movement can be observed with modern ploughing at the incomplete stage when the outside of the field (left to turn on) is yet to be ploughed; small quantities of soil are dragged from the furrow on to the stubble. Over the years, with the repetitive pattern of open-field ploughing, these small quantities built up to form substantial heaps at the end of each land; they were called *heads* or *butts* and are most important archaeologically (fig. 4).

Triangular-shaped lands, which occur occasionally in order to fill in odd areas, were called *gores*. Lands subsequently allowed to grass over were known as *leys*.

Groups of lands with the furrows running parallel were called *furlongs*. This term must not be confused with the modern meaning; it referred to an area, not a length. Each furlong had a name, and it will be seen that these names are of considerable historical and topographical importance. The size of a furlong depended on the terrain. Where soft soil was cut into by a multiplicity of watercourses and small valleys (which were called *slades* or *dales),* furlongs would have been small. On gentle terrains furlongs were very long, each comprising several hundred lands. Where two furlongs had furrows lying at right angles to each other, the first land of one furlong, which was made up of the heads of all the lands in the other furlong, was known as a *headland* (figs. 3, 5). Furlong boundaries with lands running at right angles to them on either side were made up of a double row of heads and were called *joints* (figs. 3, 6). In the late medieval period narrow lands were allowed to grass over and became used as common permanent rights of way, called *balks*.

Fig. 1. Ridge and furrow east of Yelvertoft (**SP** 6075). (Cambridge University Collection, copyright reserved.)

Fig. 2. Ridge and furrow at Castle Ashby (SP 868608).

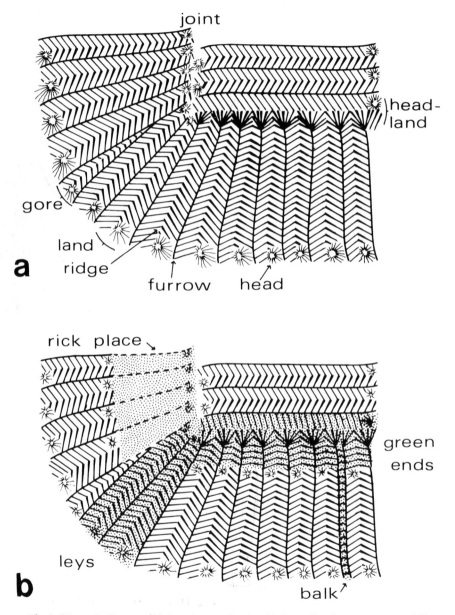

Fig. 3. Schematic diagram of furlong layout, showing **(a)** the medieval arrangement, and **(b)** later modifications with addition of grassed down areas (stippled).

Fig. 4. Small mounds of soil called 'heads' deposited by ploughing action at the end of each strip. Wollaston (SP 903634).

For purposes of crop rotation and, in the Midland region, for communal grazing of fallow land, furlongs were often grouped together into two or three large blocks called *fields*. More will be said about these later.

The *meadows* (i.e. permanent pastures lying near rivers and streams that were subject to winter flooding) were also divided into strips. These were called by various names such as *rood, dole, pole* or *hide*. As they were not ploughed, no trace of any divisions can now be seen on the ground, except for the occasional artificial drainage ditch marking one meadow off from another.

Dating of field systems

Concerning the antiquity of surviving ridge and furrow, various controversies have arisen in the past with some writers claiming that ridge and furrow is the result of nineteenth-century steam ploughing. Beresford suggested, in 1957, that most ridge and furrow had pre-enclosure origins but as late as 1973 it was claimed that there was little evidence to support this. However, even a cursory comparison of an open-field plan and vertical aerial photographs shows that the correspondence of the historical evidence and the evidence on the ground

Fig. 5. A headland, at the boundary between two furlongs with strips lying at right angles. Castle Ashby (SP 867609).

Fig. 6. The boundary between two furlongs with strips lying in the same orientation, called a joint. Wollaston (SP 903634).

Fig. 7. Steam-plough ridge and furrow at Naseby (nineteenth century) (SP 688787).

is normally exact.

Detailed comparisons have been made for eighteen parishes with surviving pre-enclosure plans in Oxfordshire, Cambridgeshire, Bedfordshire and Northamptonshire and in all cases the agreement is precise. It is clear, therefore, that ridge and furrow is at least as old as the earliest maps; the finest one so far encountered is that for Strixton, Northamptonshire, dated 1583.

Victorian steam-plough ridge and furrow does exist; good examples can be seen at King's Cliffe (TL 014993). In this case there is no doubt about the date; an area of medieval Rockingham Forest was cleared, enclosed and ploughed in the mid nineteenth century. The lands are very wide (about 14 metres, 15 yards), and the furrows quite straight and parallel to the new hedges; these lands are quite unlike the small curved medieval strips. Other examples can be found at Shenington, Oxfordshire, and in many parts of Warwickshire. Fig. 7 shows an example at Naseby.

A glance at most grass ridge and furrow fields in the Midlands will show that the present (i.e. enclosure) hedges are set over the furlongs, no matter how old the enclosure, whether fifteenth or nineteenth century, suggesting that the ridge and furrow must be at least as old as the fifteenth century.

Historically ridge and furrow patterns can be shown to be medieval where there are detailed surveys with furlong names corresponding to those on open-field maps. This has been done for Wollaston, where

Fig. 8. Manorial boundary ditch, 1231, with ridge and furrow. Wollaston (SP 905623).

lengthy terriers of 1372 and 1430 list most of the furlong names marked on a map of 1774. All the furlong boundaries shown on this map survive on the ground. Few such detailed studies appear to have been published, although it is easy enough to find names from late medieval documents that correspond to furlong names on the open-field maps, implying that most cases would be like that at Wollaston with a long-term continuity.

Earlier examples of dated field systems can be worked out; Kislingbury, for instance, has a detailed survey of every strip in 1611, which gives the furlong names. St Andrew's Priory, Northampton, held some of this land and a minutely detailed account was made in the fourteenth century. The names correspond closely, and since the grant of land was made to the priory in the early twelfth century it is reasonable to assume that the whole of Kislingbury's open fields was extant at this early period.

There is physical evidence showing that some ridge and furrow is medieval, the best known being Hen Domen, Montgomery, Powys, where ridges are buried by eleventh-century earthworks. At Bentley Grange, South Yorkshire, mining spoil heaps of the twelfth century overlie ridge and furrow. Various other dated medieval features cut across, or through, pieces of ridge and furrow, unequivocally demonstrating that these areas are ancient. At Titchmarsh a manorial garden was enlarged to include part of a furlong. On the inner side the lands can still be seen in their low-profile thirteenth-century state, and on the outside the remaining half lands were ploughed until 1778, forming a new series of heads abutting the park pale. Another example is again at Wollaston; a document of 1231 describes the garden bounds of one of the two manors, stating that it stretched as far as a ditch dug anciently through ploughland. The earthworks of this manor survive intact and the ditch can still be seen curving through low-profile ridges (fig. 8). These lands are twelfth-century at the latest, if 'ancient' in the document can be assumed to mean older than thirty-one years.

Thus it is not difficult to show that various pieces of ridge and furrow are medieval and, where detailed studies have been made, furlong names on open-field maps can be shown to date back to the fourteenth and fifteenth centuries, and in some cases to the twelfth century. The overall physical layout of open fields must therefore have changed but little from this period until enclosure.

Historical sources

There are various sources of information on open fields. The most complete are those detailed surveys that describe every single land in a given parish or township, often called *field books, town books* or *parish terriers*. Usually they take each furlong and state the size of each strip and record the owner's name; sometimes more information is given, such as the status of the land (e.g. *demesne,* the land attached to the manor), or occasionally very detailed measurements of the areas and widths of the strips. The whole parish is thus described, listing up to six thousand holdings, depending on its size.

Field books can survive from any period up to enclosure. One of the finest medieval ones known is for the west fields of Cambridge (fourteenth century); two fifteenth-century examples are known for Northamptonshire (fig. 9). More frequent are sixteenth- and seventeenth-century field books.

Common forms of later documents are the *terriers* of glebe land or other small holdings (from the Latin *terra,* land), which describe the whereabouts of the lands in terms of the furlong referenced to neighbours on either side; there may be abuttals and cardinal directions also.

The earliest documents are the charters or deeds of grant and such like made when land changed hands from the twelfth century onwards. They often include in them some terrier type information, identifying the strip location in terms of fields, furlongs and neighbouring landholders. Deeds of the sixteenth to eighteenth centuries frequently have terriers included in them.

Details of the regulation of open fields are recorded in manorial court rolls, and information about work service, cropping procedures and yields can be deduced from the returns of manorial accounts

Fig. 9 (a). Part of the field book of Muscott, describing each strip, 1433.

Between balake putte and village
Lord of Brockhall	½acre
Agnes Brockhall	½a
Thomas Alyn	½a
Thomas Gervase	½a
James de Muscott	½a
Agnes Brockhall	½a
Thomas Gervase	½a
John Smyth	½a

Above blake putte on ye west syde
John Heyford	1 rood butt
John Smyth	1 r butt
Nicholas Malyn	1 r butt
Thomas Williams	1 r butt
James de Muscott	½ r butt
Thomas Clerke	½ a butt
John Heyford	1 r butt
John Smyth	1 r butt
Thomas Gervase	½ a butt

Grethers begynnyng on ye west syde
Lord of Brockhall	1½r
Thomas Alyn	1½r
Lord of Brockhall	1a
over the balke	
Thomas Clerke	1a
John Heyford	½a
John Smyth	½a
Thomas Gervase	1a
Lord of Brockhall	½a
John Smyth	½a
Richard Malyn	½a
John Hurles	½a
John Smyth	½a
John Ward	½a

Lord of Brockhall	1a
John Heyford	½a
Jn. Smith of Brockhall	½a
Thomas Gervase	1a
Lord of Brockhall	½a
John Smyth	½a
John Ward	½a
John Smyth	½a
James de Muscott	1a
Thomas Clerke	1a
John Heyford	½a
John Smyth	½a
Thomas Gervase	1½a

Under chyrche wey begynnyng on ye sowth syde
Lord of Brockhall	½a
Thomas Gervase	1a
John Smyth of Brockhall	½a
John Heyford	½a
Lord of Brockhall	1a
William Chapelyn	½a
James de Muscott	½a
John Hurles	½a
Nicholas Malyn	½a
John Smyth	½a
Lord of Brockhall	½a
which is a headland	

Flynteborough in ye water on ye est syde
James de Malyn	½a
Agnes Brockhall	½a
Nicholas Malyn	½a
John Smyth	½a

Fig. 9 (b). Translation of fig. 9 (a).

Fig. 10. Part of Strixton open-field map, 1591 copy of 1583. The area north of the village is enclosed and shows no ridge and furrow (SP 902618).

from the thirteenth century onwards.

From the 1580s there exist for some parishes estate plans showing the layout of the open fields and the tenurial arrangements (fig. 10). Frequently they are not a complete account of the medieval landscape because of contraction of the ploughing area and the establishment of closes left as permanent pasture.

Published accounts are available which detail the type of historical records that survive and explain what kind of information can be recovered.

2
The operation of open fields

Open-field farming was a communal affair. The amount of land attached to a peasant holding was called a *virgate* or *yardland,* and in northern counties an *oxgang* or *bovate.* Its size could vary from 7 to 16 hectares (17 to 40 acres) depending on the region; small acreages are typical of intensively cultivated parishes with no marginal land. The yardland consisted of the appropriate number of individual lands or strips (between forty and eighty) scattered throughout a given parish in most or all of the furlongs. There were thus no two lands lying together belonging to the same man, provided he held one yardland only. In this way all parts of the parish, good soil and bad soil alike, were shared out amongst the village community. The number of yardlands varied, approximately relating to parish size; thus the small (now deserted) village of Muscott consisted of nineteen yardlands and the Nene valley parish of Ecton had 103.

The farming of these scattered holdings had, therefore, to be a communal matter. Clearly it would not be possible, in the same furlong, for some lands to be under a corn crop and other adjacent ones to be left fallow for grazing. As there were no fences animals would naturally damage the standing corn and so it was essential for the whole village to arrange a regular cycle of crop rotation and fallow grazing.

In the Midland region it was probably the need to regulate grazing that precipitated organised communal arrangements for running the open fields. Most of the area is of reasonably fertile low-lying soil which can be cultivated, and which encouraged intensive settlement by the early medieval period with its associated arable land. At an early date the arable would begin to encroach upon the meadow and marginal land which was needed to feed both stock and draught animals. The solution of this problem was to allow animals to feed on fallow lands and stubble after harvest. Such an arrangement demanded that the fallow always be in a compact block; in this way animals were easily controlled and kept off those furlongs used for crops. These large areas were called *fields.* Typically there were two or three fields supporting a two or three year crop rotation.

Another immediate consequence of such a system was that the individual peasant holdings which comprised the yardland had to be uniformly distributed throughout the fields. This ensured that there were always some lands under cultivation: if the distribution was irregular then there would be danger that in one year all the lands

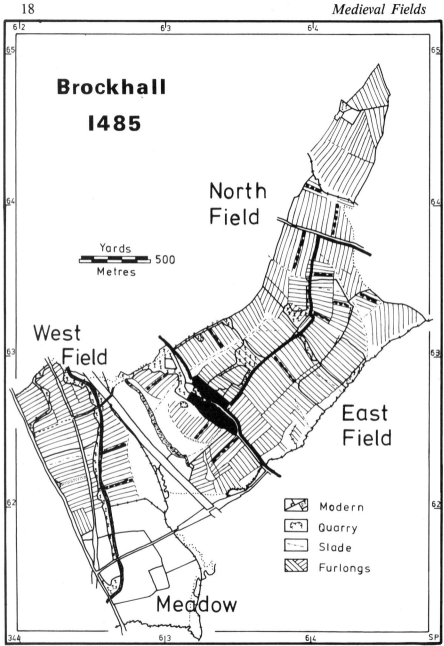

Brockhall

1485

North
Field

Yards
500
Metres

West
Field

East
Field

Modern
Quarry
Slade
Furlongs

Meadow

Fig. 11. Brockhall three-field system in 1485 (SP 6362).

could lie in the fallow field and there would be no yield of corn or other produce. Fig. 11 shows the layout of Brockhall in 1485.

Two features, then, were unique to the two- and three-field system: the use of the fallow for common grazing, and the equal distribution of lands between the fields. This last feature comes out clearly in most charters and terriers. Fig. 12 details a small grant of land at Brockhall in 1483; the fields are not specified in this case, but each single land is plotted on fig. 11 (broken lines).

The communal attitude to land holding is brought out by valuations of manorial estates upon the death of the lord. At Kislingbury, in 1360, it is stated that two-thirds of the lord's cornland was valued at £3 and the remaining third was worth nothing, because it was fallow and lay in common. This is a very different attitude from today when fallow land certainly would be valued in an assessment of property.

Communal regulations also extended to the meadows and the number of animals that could be kept for each yardland. Possession of a yardland automatically implied rights in the meadow: the actual acreage varied enormously depending upon the available meadow in a given township. Thus if there were eighty yardlands of arable a single holding would have about one eightieth of the meadow, also scattered in strips. Most meadows were kept free of animals until hay was taken from the individual strips, after which communal grazing was allowed for the rest of the season. Some meadows had their strips allocated by lottery and were called *dole meadows*.

The number of animals that could be adequately kept was regulated at an early date. At Cold Ashby, in 1231, the Abbot of Pipewell Abbey (near Kettering) and the lord of the manor agreed that there should be, for each of sixty yardlands, four beasts (oxen, cows etc), four pigs and twenty-four sheep.

Gray, in 1915, was the first to define the 'Midland system', in the area where the two- and three-field system predominated. The three-field system is seen as a development of the two-field method. If there were a continued increase in population (and so the need for more crops), a three-field arrangement would allow more land to be cropped in one year than a two-field system. In the most densely settled parts of the region the change was occurring in the thirteenth century: Thornby had a two-field arrangement in *c* 1230 but neighbouring Naseby was three-field by *c* 1290.

On the fringes of the region many two-field systems, once set up, remained unchanged throughout their history until enclosure. Fox has published examples of the remodelling of irregular field systems: at Dry Drayton, Cambridgeshire, a three-field arrangement was made in

Fig. 12. Brockhall charter describing 1.4 hectares (3½ acres) lying in fourteen parcels, 1483. Freely translated it reads: 'Richard Waldyng of Brokhole confirms to Thomas Smyth of Brokhole and to William Smyth, 3½ acres of arable land in the fields of Brokhole; of which 1 rood lies beyond *le strete* next to the land of Jylys, 1 rood lies in *aschbroke* next to land of Starton, 1 rood abuts *le strete* next Thomas Smyth, 1 rood at *gardeswell* next to the lord, 1 rood in *hangyng lond* next to Starton, another rood in *hangyng lond* next to the land of Sulby, 1 rood in *crosdale* next to Thomas Smyth, another rood in *crosdale* next to Jylys, 1 rood upon *clippe* next to the lord, 1 rood with a head in *stanwell* next to the lord, 1 rood abutting upon the *pynfold* next to the lord, 1 rood abutting in *le lake* next to the lord, 1 rood abutting in *sichbroke* with a head next to the lord, another rood with head in *sychbroke* next to the land of Mychell : . . . . . witnessed by John Smyth of Muscote, Edward Peterlyng, Richard Pryd, Simon Alen, William Aton. Date, at Brokhole, 23rd August 1 Richard III.

c 1150, and at Segenhoe, Bedfordshire, a two-field system was created in the 1160s. Normally the creation of regular fields would have occurred before there was any detailed historical record.

In other parts of Britain irregular field systems prevailed, with the landholders' strips not uniformly distributed throughout the fields. The terms 'furlong' and 'field' were used indiscriminately, mainly for locational purposes, and there was not any discernible method of communal crop rotation. Such irregular fields were a feature of East Anglia and east Cambridgeshire. In most cases there was plenty of grazing waste land, either on sandy heaths or boulder clay left as permanent pasture. Parts of the sandy Breckland were sometimes taken into cultivation for a brief period and then left for grazing to replenish the fertility. Herds from the grassland were folded on the demesne to manure it.

Kent is another region that was quite different from the Midlands. Here the units of peasant land, called *yokelands,* were originally held in a compact block and farmed independently. The later fragmentation of these holdings, equally between heirs, caused some dispersal, but there was never anything akin to the three-field system.

In the Celtic areas other very different systems operated. Scotland practised the infield and outfield method, which was based on the farm rather than the village, so that areas involved were usually small (up to 200 hectares, 500 acres). Near the farmstead was an area known as the *infield* (about one fifth of the total area), which was continuously cultivated using a threefold or fourfold rotation. There was no fallow, fertility being maintained by manuring. The remainder of the estate was called the *outfield* and received no manure. It was ploughed perhaps for about five successive years and then left to revert to grass for a long period. All the arable was divided into ridges, similar to those in England, but the arrangement was called *run-rig* (fig. 13). Strips were often reallocated each year. An additional feature for most Scottish farmsteads was the large area of waste beyond the field systems where animals could graze in the summer.

Some idea of the nature of agriculture in the Midland region can be deduced from the account rolls of medieval estates. The yields of grain and seed were very low. Wellingborough manorial accounts give the quantities of seed set and harvested. In 1259 and 1292 the yields were between three and six times the quantities sown — a paltry return compared with that of up to fortyfold which is obtained today. Similar figures are available for Rushden and Higham Ferrers for 1314, where the yield for pease was 2.4, oats 2.7 and wheat 3.1

Fig. 13. Scottish ridge and furrow (run-rig) near Aberdeen (NJ 848153).

times the quantities sown, all of them very meagre returns. The quantities sown per unit area were 92 kilograms per hectare (2.67 bushels per acre) for pease, 125 (4.52) for oats and 71 (2.36) for wheat.

Plott's description of Oxfordshire for the post-medieval period is very comprehensive (1676). Many of the practices described are likely to have remained unchanged since the late medieval period.

The fallow lands were ploughed soon after the beginning of May by 'casting the tilth' down from the ridge to the furrow, i.e. going around the land in an anticlockwise direction. Later in the summer ridging up in the normal way was done at least twice for each 'casting'. Clay land was ridged up more steeply than other kinds of soil for better drainage. Red land (ironstone soil) was fallowed early or late in the season, so that it did not become too dried-out. For land to be sown with wheat and barley, three or four fallowings were made.

The usual crop cycle for three-field parishes was: wheat – pease and beans – fallow. The seed was sown by broadcasting, covering a strip in a bout, i.e. one side in one direction and the other on the return journey. Harrowing the lands immediately after sowing covered the seeds.

Wheat was cut with a sickle and left in handfuls to dry out partially, before being tied into sheaves, which were set up in shocks of ten, rafter-fashion in lean-to pairs, to complete ripening. Fig. 14 illustrates a field of shocks being set up. Although taken much later than the demise of the open fields, the photograph gives a good idea of the aspect at harvest time. Barley was left in swathes and then dried by making into cocks using a trident-shaped fork (fig. 15). Beans were harvested similarly to barley, but the loose stalks and pods, left after carrying, were gleaned up, instead of being raked, so as to reduce the loss of seed.

Seven kinds of wheat were grown in the early eighteenth century, red and white Lammas wheats being the most common. Two types of barley were grown, sprat barley and long-eared barley.

Plott gives the level of sowing in the seventeenth century as about 63 kilograms per hectare (2 bushels per acre). This is very much below the modern quantity of 157 kilograms per hectare ($1\frac{1}{4}$ hundredweight per acre). Even by the end of the eighteenth century, after one and a half centuries of scientific agricultural experimentation, the maximum yields of grain were only ten or eleven fold; for example at Little Oakley in 1776 the yield of barley was 503 kilograms per hectare (4 hundredweight per acre).

Such a complex communal system of agriculture would obviously require some form of regulation. This was done through the manorial court. The manor court was the central institution of medieval village

Fig. 14. Harvesting wheat by hand.
Fig. 15. Barley, cocked to dry.

life. Each lord of a manor held a court by right, and attendance (suit of court) by the villeins, tenants and freeholders was obligatory. The court was chiefly administrative, organising the running of the open fields, appointing local officers and applying the manorial customs. The judicial matters dealt with were mainly restricted to conditions of tenancy, services and dues within the manor. The misdemeanours and rights of the tenants are recorded, so giving quite a detailed account of the lives of ordinary villagers. Originally courts were held every few weeks, but gradually they became less frequent.

The courts appointed officers to control various aspects of the open fields. The hayward was in charge of the common herd and had to prevent it from trespassing on to crops or meadow. Any stray cattle were placed in a pound in the centre of the village, and a fine had to be paid before they were released.

Cattle were taken daily from the farmsteads in the village to the grazing area and back again at night. By the seventeenth century villagers had to send boys along to help.

Gradually courts began to record the various customs of each manor or township. The thirteenth-century regulations for numbers of cattle at Cold Ashby have already been noted; other orders are recorded in increasing numbers with the passage of time. Newton Longville and Great Horwood, both in Buckinghamshire, have good series of orders dating from the early fourteenth century.

A full set of orders, dated 1577, for Brixworth includes a wide variety of regulations. For example, the number of animals per yardland and their physical whereabouts were controlled. No separate private herd could be kept, all animals being part of the common herd during the day, and returned to the village farmsteads at night. The dates of hay cutting, breaking up fallow land and so on were all regulated, and so were the rights of gleaning. Most of such orders were of great antiquity even though not written down in detail until relatively late.

3
Methods of reconstruction of open-field plans

In order satisfactorily to interpret documentary evidence and study the precise layout of medieval estates, it is essential to have a plan of the open fields (i.e. a furlong plan). Some counties are well endowed with plans from 1580 onwards, and others are not. In most cases the plans are inadequate because there will have been a contraction of the arable land since the medieval period, some areas of former subdivided fields being marked as 'close' or 'pasture' without any detail (see fig. 10). It is, however, possible to reconstruct open-field furlong patterns by archaeological techniques.

Fieldwork techniques

In a permanent-grass modern field containing ridge and furrow two features are instantly striking: the undulating ridges themselves and the high banks of plough-moved soil that form the furlong boundaries (the headlands and joints). Both are easy to identify and survey.

When a ridged field is ploughed flat in the modern way not all traces disappear; the positions of the ridges are still visible (for fifty years or more, depending on the soil) as light and dark subsoil marks; and the piled-up ends of the strips (heads) are not much flattened but remain smoothed together as a linear bank of soil. Thus wherever a group of strips met another set, either orientated in the same direction or at right angles, there will remain a bank of soil when the whole area is ploughed out. A survey of these banks in an entire parish allows the complete pattern of strip groupings (furlongs) to be determined. Care must be taken when examining a modern arable field not to confuse the results of modern ploughing with the older earthworks. However, ancient features are generally too large to be mistaken for modern ones; some soil banks are very broad, especially on gravel soils, and are often confused with Roman roads by the inexperienced. They can be as much as 50 metres (55 yards) wide and 1 metre (1 yard) high in the middle.

Surveys are easiest to make in spring when fields have been worked smooth. It is often convenient to begin in a permanent-grass field containing undisturbed strip ridges and boundaries. Banks in arable fields are often easier to observe when rows of young corn emerge (fig. 16).

Fig. 16. Ploughed-over furlong boundary (AA) surviving as a bank of soil. Strixton (SP 897623).

Actual strips can often be seen surviving as soil marks, particularly in fields ploughed for the first time in the modern way during 1940-5. Aerial photographs (especially those taken by the Royal Air Force in the 1940s) are useful supplements to ground surveys, since strips may show as crop marks; however, the linear banks are not usually visible from the air. Parishes which were enclosed before about 1725 frequently have hedges set along furlong boundaries; differences in soil levels between modern fields and changes in the orientation of the strips have to be sought.

Having arranged for access to a whole parish, and equipped with a clipper board and copies of the appropriate 1:10,000 (or 6 inches to the mile) Ordnance Survey maps, one can easily record all the furlong boundaries. Furlong maps with an accurate indication of the strip orientation can be prepared. Plans of the type of fig. 11 make no attempt to represent the exact number of lands: it would be impossible to reduce the plan to a convenient size, and in any case it is very rare to discover a parish in which all the strip widths could now be determined, either on the ground or by aerial photography. Approximately one strip in four is represented on the reconstructions.

The fieldwork techniques are not limited to those parts of the country where ridge and furrow was practised. The movement of soil

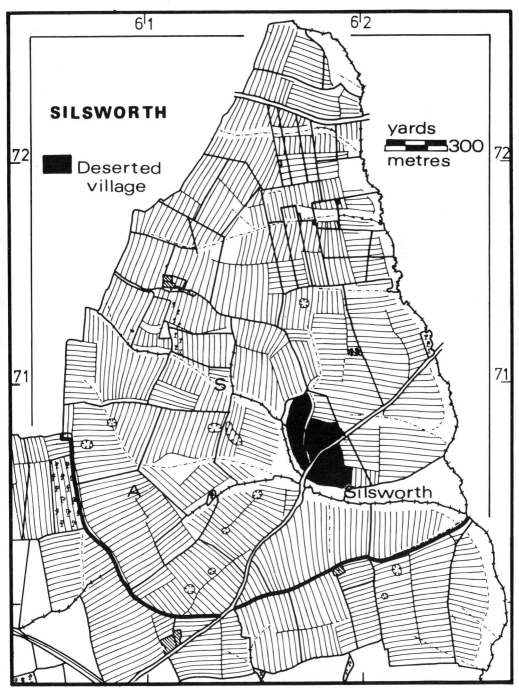

Fig. 17. Silsworth deserted village and estate boundary (SP 6170).

to the furlong boundary, i.e. the turning point, still occurred with flat ploughing. In the Chippenham and Burwell areas of Cambridgeshire furlong boundaries can be mapped very easily because of their large size, even though there was never any ridge and furrow in this region.

Furlong boundaries are more developed in those Midland areas that received the longest ploughing, i.e. those which were the latest to be enclosed. Geology also affects the size: boundary banks on light soils tend to be easily dispersed by modern ploughing. Heavy clay yields boundaries that survive well enough, but often they were not greatly developed in the first place. Thus in many north Bedfordshire parishes the heavy clay soil was woodland and pasture until ploughed up in the late thirteenth century; by the fifteenth century, after the decrease of population and contraction of arable area, these lands were the first to be left as permanent pasture or enclosed. The best soils seem to be the clayey loams that developed over Jurassic clays and limestones and on Cretacious marls.

Problems are met when regions further from the Midlands are studied. Thus the techniques are more difficult to apply on the Yorkshire Wolds, where there are light soils and few furlong boundaries. In most parts of Wales and Scotland there was rarely sufficient area or depth of soil to allow an extensive network of boundaries to form.

Once the furlong pattern has been established, the general layout of the medieval countryside will be apparent. For those parishes most intensively cultivated the furlongs will include nearly all the available area, leaving but little room by brooks and rivers for the communal pasture. In other areas there may have been some moor, heath, fen or woodland remaining. Where the present village has not expanded in recent centuries the exact extent of the medieval settlement will be apparent from the earthworks.

Applications

Sometimes furlong patterns reveal ancient boundaries of which the whereabouts have long been forgotten. Many parishes include more than one ancient estate; some of them had separate open-field systems. The case of Watford (Northamptonshire) is a good example. It consisted of four manors: the main settlement with church is Watford; attached to it was Cumberford; to the east lies the shrunken settlement of Murcott and to the north is the deserted village of Silsworth. This last has an early origin (Middle Saxon pottery has been found there) and a distinct and separate open-field arrangement. The lordship boundary is very clear in the furlong patterns (fig. 17).

Another case is the township boundary of West Cotton and Mallows Cotton. These deserted villages now lie in the parishes of

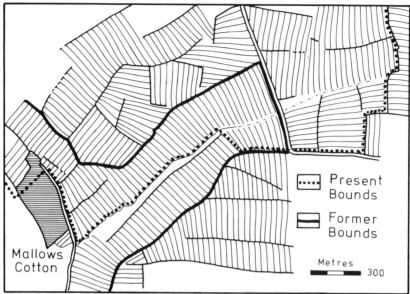

Fig. 18. The lordship boundary of Mallows Cotton showing in the furlong pattern (SP 980733).

Raunds and Ringstead respectively, but once they formed a separate estate. The original boundary shows very clearly in the furlong pattern. In fig. 18 the thick line represents a discontinuity which is best explained by its being an ancient boundary.

The identification of the furlongs and any other topographical features is essential if historical data are to be properly understood. When no open-field plan with named furlongs exists it is often a difficult and challenging task but well worth the effort.

Initially all topographical names recorded on maps and plans must be collected on a copy of the 1:10,000 map. Enclosure maps (i.e. plans made when the medieval fields ceased to be used and the 'modern' hedges were planted) usually give a few names. More useful are eighteenth- and nineteenth-century plans of enclosed estates and tithe maps, which normally give the field names, acreage and cultivation. Not to be overlooked are sale catalogues, which frequently contain plans with field names. Even though they may only refer to a small part of a parish they can be significant because sufficient numbers may exist to account for a larger area. Many county record offices have collections of field names made during the last sixty years. Northamptonshire has a set compiled by schoolchildren in 1932 as part of the preparation for the 1933 county Place Name

Society volume. They are very useful, but allowance should be made for the names to be a field or so away from their true location. This arose because in some cases neither the children nor the aged farmworker who was usually consulted were adept at reading maps. In fig. 19b the modern field names for part of the parish of Ashby St Ledgers are shown and are compared with identified furlong names (fig. 19a).

The next stage is to collect together the historical data in tabular form. A list of furlong names is prepared, grouped together in the fields. If a field book exists then the number of lands in each furlong is added up and recorded on the list. Most medieval terriers state the name of the occupier either side (see fig. 12):

'one land in Riggeway furlong John Robinson on the west and the lord on the east, and abutting Brington meer.'

From this it is obvious that the lands in the furlong lie north-south and that Riggeway furlong is on the edge of the parish next to the neighbouring lordship of Brington. Some terriers and field books give detailed abuttals, e.g. 'Long Cold Ditch furlong shooting to Little Cold Ditch (furlong) east and London road west; Short Cold Ditch furlong shooting to Moores east and Long Cold Ditch west; Spittle Wall furlong shooting to Hades north and Little Cold Ditch south; Mansell furlong shooting to Spittle Wall north and Long Cold Ditch south'. From this a series of furlongs can easily be related to each other.

All surviving documents are searched for locational data and the detail is added to the table. The required information is then readily accessible.

The actual furlong identification is now possible by combining the evidence from all three sources, i.e. the reconstructed furlong map, the map of field names, and the table of furlong data (fig. 19).

In clear-cut cases such as Ashby St Ledgers, where there is a field book, a good set of post-enclosure field names and plenty of furlong abuttals, it is an easy matter to start from a known point on the parish boundary and plot the furlongs directly on to the 1:10,560 plan. On this scale lands of an average of 7 metres width are 0.7 millimetres wide.

In a more typical area where the data are not so good, a slightly different procedure has to be adopted. A strip of thin cardboard no more than 20 millimetres ($\frac{3}{4}$ inch) wide is marked off in 'furlongs' measured to scale. These are then cut up, the name of the furlong written on with any abuttal information and the land orientation. It is then possible to arrange and rearrange these 'furlongs' on the reconstructed plan until they form a reasonable interpretation of all the evidence.

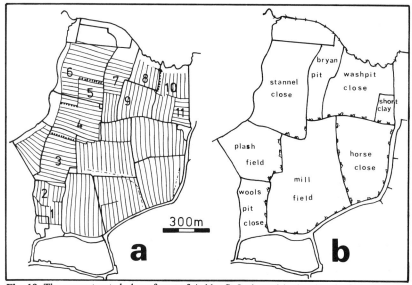

Fig. 19. The reconstructed plan of part of Ashby St Ledgers **(a)**, showing the furlong names identified using the field names of 1808 **(b)**, and data from a field book *(below)*. (SP 5768.)

PART OF FEDDY FIELD

name		orientation of lands	number of lands	notes
1	Woolspitt	NS	31	
2	Woolspitt leys	NS	10 + 'piece'	
3	Plash	EW	39	headland south, part headlands north
4	Longbreach	EW	24	
5	Just poles	EW	24	
6	Stanwell hill	EW	16 + 28 leys	
7	Costydene	EW	17 + 28 leys	
8	Costy hill	NS	21	headland west
9	Hanging woolsbreach	NS	58	shooting horse close
10	Washpit leys	NS	20	
11	Short clay	EW	18	headland north

The reconstructed plans can be used to present various forms of historical data. The simplest kind is to illustrate the land use at a given period.

Ashby St Ledgers has a field book of 1715 which distinguishes between arable and land set down to grass (i.e. ley). It also gives the fields, the meadows and (by default) the area already enclosed. A complete view of the parish is thus available at this period (fig. 20). The area to the north-west had been split off as a separate enclosed

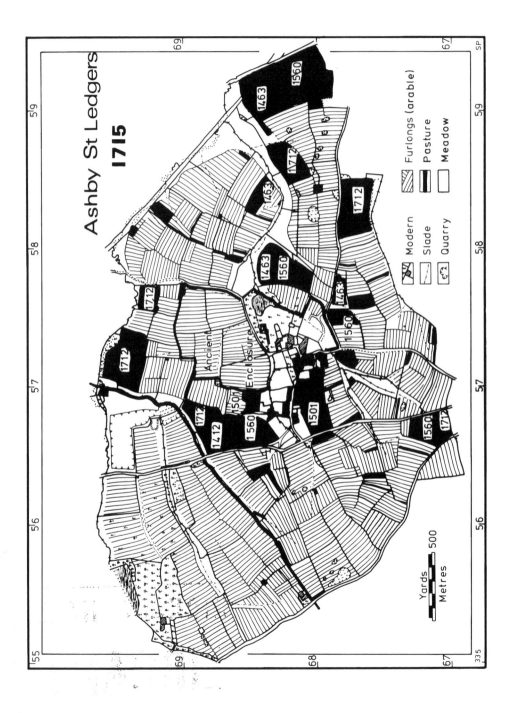

Ashby St Ledgers
1715

Furlongs (arable)

Modern
Slade
Quarry

Pasture

Meadow

Ancient Enclosure

Yards 500
Metres

estate before 1519. Some encroachment of closes on the former arable lands is evident around the village. A considerable amount of grass had been established in the open fields to supplement the grass of the meadows.

The precise layout of ancient estates can be plotted on the plans. Historical data are frequently available about the location of the demesne (the land farmed directly by the lord of the manor). In the case of Hardingstone, the lord of the manor in 1660 (William Tate) held parcels of four lands lying next to each other, each parcel occurring at regular intervals throughout all the furlongs.

Not all cases are as uniform as this. At Ashby St Ledgers and Kislingbury some of the demesne was in blocks near the centre of the village in *c* 1210 and *c* 1110 respectively. However, in later centuries, there seems to have been a more uniform distribution of the demesne. Thus Brockhall, East Haddon (fig. 21) and Flore are exactly like Hardingstone, with small groups of lands lying fairly uniformly distributed.

The above examples illustrate new techniques of identifying early estates. The field books give detailed and precise information about ownership of land, generally in the sixteenth and seventeenth centuries. However, the data can readily be extrapolated back in time in the case of monastic lands. It is generally known at what date a given holding or estate was granted to a religious house, and also who received the land after the dissolution. It is thus relatively simple to work out which owner in the field book held the former monastic land and so identify the early estate that had been granted. In the case of Kislingbury there is a field book of 1611 and, unusually, a very detailed fourteenth-century terrier, already mentioned. The land given was part of the grantors' demesne.

Such precise detail is not possible without a field book but as long as there are good terriers available the appropriate furlong locations can normally be identified and estates can be approximately located on the ground.

Topographical history, i.e. changing land use, is deducible from the furlong names themselves. Land taken in from former woodland (*assarted*) often had furlong names such as *wold, stocking, stibbings, haw* etc. As in many cases these names can be traced back to the thirteenth century it is clear that the woodland must have been older still, i.e. probably late Saxon in origin.

Larger units of ancient landscape can be observed when several ad-

Fig. 20. *(Left)* Ashby St Ledgers land use in 1715. The dates of the grassland are the earliest recorded for each given piece (SP 5768).

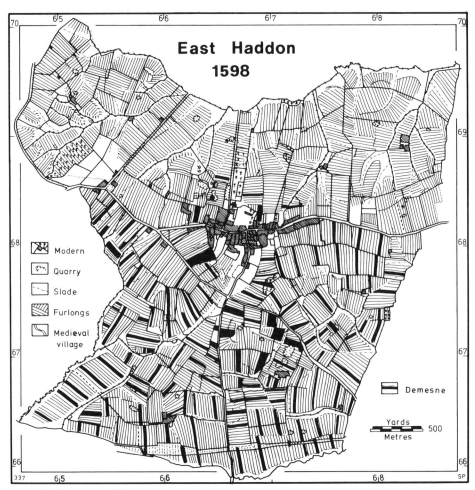

Fig. 21. East Haddon manorial land (demesne) in 1598 (SP 6768).

jacent parishes are examined. Finedon, Burton Latimer, Cranford St John, Woodford, Great and Little Addington all have *wold* furlong names in remote parts of the parishes that are all contiguous. The area is conterminous with an outcrop of heavy boulder clay and almost certainly represents an ancient woodland. Although such terrain was not initially preferred and cleared for agricultural land, it nevertheless was a valuable resource, for woodland products, grazing and so on. The communities of the seven parishes each demanded access and had their own part, Woodford parish having a long 'tongue' to get at the wood.

There are similar cases of furlong names recalling former marginal land. An area common to the lordships of Whilton, Muscott, Brockhall and Brington was once rough moor lying on wet clayey

Fig. 22. Parishes sharing former marginal moorland, in some cases by having long extensions from the village centres (SP 6464).

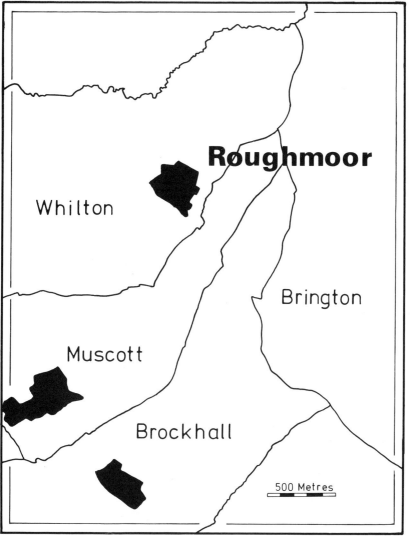

ground (fig. 22). Muscott and Brockhall have long 'tongues' stretching to the moor, demonstrating its importance in the village economy.

In some cases there are historical references to the process of the addition of peripheral lands into the open fields. At Cold Ashby in *c* 1230 the Abbot of Pipewell complained that the local lord, Eustace de Watford, had ploughed a furlong next to the road to Welford which used to be part of *Syfletemor* common pasture. Often such processes were complete before there was any detailed record, and the furlong names themselves are the only evidence.

By these means the reconstruction of the furlong patterns enables the historical record to be clearly interpreted and leads to the identification of early estates, land use and details of topography.

Fig. 23. Brixworth, showing grassland created in the open fields by 1688 (SP 7570).

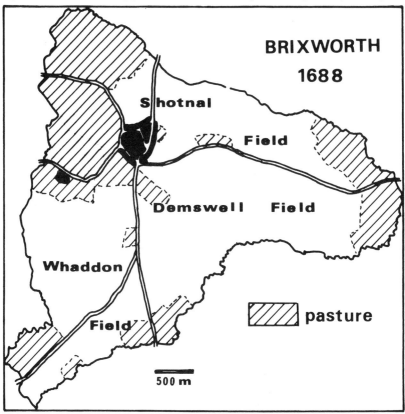

4
Later modifications
of field systems

The mature two- or three-field systems that had been established by the thirteenth century were modified in many ways in the post-medieval period. Some changes resulted from a declining population and others occurred by deliberate variation of agricultural practice.

Medieval population was at its maximum in the early decades of the fourteenth century. Thereafter, for well over a century, it declined because of continual havoc caused by disease and economic recession. By the fifteenth century there was no longer sufficient population to maintain a labour-intensive agricultural system. Lords attracted villeins from nearby manors by offering them money for work rendered, so freeing them from the feudal obligations of work service to the lord, and permanent residence in their home manor. In this way feudal society began to collapse and a free yeomanry eventually developed.

Because of the lack of labour many of the strips in the fields were left as permanent grass. These were called leys. The amount of grass created varied; sometimes odd strips, or groups of strips, were left, and sometimes whole blocks of furlongs. The areas chosen for pasture were generally those where the soil was the poorest, or if the soil quality was uniform, then the region chosen was that furthest from the village and so inconvenient to reach with a plough team. Frequently the two coincided, in that the far distant parts of the parish had originally been heavy clay forest land or dry heath. Fig. 23 shows Brixworth in 1688; the grass lies on clay.

There was regional variation from parish to parish, again usually dictated by geology. Poorer soil areas, such as East Haddon, had a greater total percentage of leys in the sixteenth century than the rich-soil Nene valley parishes, such as Higham Ferrers. All the central Nene valley lordships were noted for their corn growing in the eighteenth century.

Contemporary writers were well aware of these large-scale changes of land use. Thus, at East Haddon, it was stated in 1771: 'the cow pasture contains 600 acres of ancient greensoard that has not been plowed up for more than 500 years.' Referring to Northamptonshire in 1712 a topographical historian writes:

'Many of the Lordships, and especially the larger ones, have a

Common or uninclosed Pasture for their Cattel in the Outskirts of the Fields. Most of these have formerly been plowed; but being generally their worst sort of ground, and at so great Distance from the Towns, the Manuring and Culture of them were found so inconvenient that they have been laid down for Greensod.'

The result was a contraction of the arable land. Open-field maps of the sixteenth to nineteenth centuries rarely show details of lands in these permanent pasture areas, and for this reason many past writers have assumed that the pastures and heaths depicted were a permanent ancient feature and had never been ploughed.

It often happened that the lands allowed to revert to pasture were the same ones that had been taken into cultivation from the waste for only a few centuries. With modern intensive cultivation all remains are now being eradicated, making it difficult to reconstruct furlong patterns by fieldwork techniques in these areas.

Well documented parishes, such as Ashby St Ledgers, show that the reversion of furlongs to grass began in the fifteenth century and continued throughout the sixteenth and seventeenth. In this parish there was a further considerable increase made in 1712 by a new manorial owner (fig. 20).

Such large-scale changes must have necessitated some rearrangement of the extent of the two or three fields so that equality of size was maintained.

Open-field arable was also encroached upon by enclosures, i.e. the creation of what we would now call 'fields', by setting a hedge around a given plot. The land so enclosed was usually left as pasture. Most commonly such enclosures were made adjacent to the village, so that some or all of the landholders had a paddock of permanent grass next to their croft or homestead. This was convenient for raising breeding stock.

Sometimes the larger pasture areas of the type first discussed were also hedged in as a close; for example, on the periphery of Brockhall and Muscott, 40 hectares (100 acres) were enclosed as pasture in 1433.

Balks were narrow strips of grass left between some lands and were used as common access routes. From the fifteenth century balks were frequently created and were used as fixed reference points in descriptions of open-field holdings. However, the extensive series of terriers for Peterborough Abbey tenants, dating mainly from 1230 to 1320, does not mention them (except in a late example of 1340). At Strixton, in 1360, a balk called the Hullebalke existed, but it was not then a common right of way because many people were fined for using it.

Balks also served as boundary markers for significant divisions

Fig. 24. Small heads formed by leaving the ends of lands as grass. Wootton (SP 767563).

within furlongs. At Ashby St Ledgers consolidated parcels of strips, formerly part of the demesne, were marked off with balks. At Great Billing a regular cycle of forty-three strips was divided by balks into parcels of ten, thirteen and twenty. When not in use as routes, balks were used for hay and for tethering animals.

Manorial court bylaws of the post-medieval period sometimes order the setting out of private balks; for example, at Wollaston in 1633 balks were to be set out 1.2 metres (4 feet) wide between every five, six or seven roods in the Windmill Field and in Wood Field and 0.6 metres (2 feet) wide in the Nether Field. These very narrow strips or balks can still be seen. At Helmdon (SP 584417) and Naseby (SP 684787) there are furlongs with a narrow balk between every land — presumably the result of such court orders.

Another practice was to leave the end of lands unploughed so that a few metres of grass were formed. Some court rolls for Maidford specifically mention a 7 metre (8 yard) length to be left.

Where a few metres of grass were left, the plough had to have a new turning point, which, after a few years, would cause piles of soil to accumulate in the same manner as the original headlands and joints had been formed. Examples can be seen at Wootton (fig. 24) and in the parishes in the north-west of Northamptonshire such as

Fig. 25. A rick place where stacks were left in the open fields. Brixworth (SP 744692).

Clipston, Crick and Long Buckby. Each furlong boundary has a parallel row of little heads set back a few metres. If every land in every furlong was treated in this manner, then the result would have been a strip of grass left around all four sides. An example of this can be seen on the draft enclosure map of Little Houghton, of *c* 1829, which marks all the grass in the parish. Such practices explain comments like 'every furlong had a strip of grass left around it', often met in confused accounts of open fields. The increase of grass in the seventeenth century often caused such an arrangement but it was not an original feature of the layout of medieval fields.

In 1611, at Kislingbury and elsewhere, the heads or green ends often belonged to a different person from the arable strips. Heads are mentioned at a much earlier period, for example in 1235 at Thornby and 1367 at Welton, but there is no indication whether they were grass at these dates.

Another modification sometimes observed is that two furlongs with strips going in the same direction, butting together at a common boundary (joint), have been ploughed together, making the strip twice as long as usual. The new strip has a kink in the middle caused by the original reversed S shape of the two parts, and there is still a bank of soil representing the former boundary. Usually this modification is of a late date, but early examples are also known; in 1252 at Salden in the parish of Mursley, Buckinghamshire, part of a terrier states:

'Item; below Little Pusshulle [furlong], one piece of the tithe of Luffield [Priory], which furlong used to be on its own [but] now the furlong of Abswale is added to it by ploughing, thus the two furlongs have been made one that used to be divided.'

A bylaw of 1577 refers to another modification of the open fields: 'None having a rick in the field shall put any sheep or hog fed at the said rick out into the field.' The occurrence of ricks or stacks in the open fields is little known and little understood. A map of Brixworth for 1688 shows a number of rick places scattered throughout the parish. Until recently, just one of these survived in an undisturbed state in a ridge and furrow pasture field (fig. 25). It was a flattened square area of ridge and furrow about 0.1 hectare ($\frac{1}{4}$ acre) in extent. The original course of the furrows was just discernible within the square but the later ones ceased at the edge, and a series of new heads had been formed. Rick places were apparently areas where stacks were placed in the open fields. They are also known at Crick (1635) and have been observed at Naseby, Clipston and Yelvertoft.

There are cases of the changing of strip widths. Landholders with two adjacent yardland holdings (i.e. sets of strips scattered in twos) often ploughed them together as one. More rarely, when a holding was divided into two a land was split lengthways so that one new land would have been formed from furrow to ridge and the other from ridge to furrow. Both of these operations probably occurred frequently in early times, but much less commonly during the period when detailed documents survive.

Such modifications all demonstrate that open-field systems could be quite flexible in their arrangements, so as to accommodate any change that might be necessary.

Changes in agricultural procedures occurred also. Some two-field systems, which presumably were originally devised to have a two-course rotation, developed a three-course system but retained the two fields. Likewise other multi-field systems developed out of the three-field systems. For example, at Finedon three original fields were each split into three parts and the fallow one-third was no longer a contiguous block, even though a three-course crop rotation was still used. These subdivisions made for greater equality of soil types.

Towards the end of the open-field system, where it survived until the eighteenth or nineteenth centuries, there is often a multiplicity of 'field' names. This is because the word 'field' was taking over from 'furlong' and need not necessarily relate either to the number of original fields or to the crop rotation.

Improvements in cropping techniques became widespread from the late seventeenth century and encouraged the changeover from open-field to enclosed-field husbandry, where new owners could experiment with their own farming, unhindered by the inefficient methods of their open-field neighbours. The many eighteenth-century publications and the returns of the Board of Agriculture, *c* 1790-1810, can be consulted for the details.

Fig. 26. Etton (Cambridgeshire), showing a rectangular field system on a flat landscape. To the north-west an early Saxon site has been ploughed over and ignored by later strips (TF 1306).

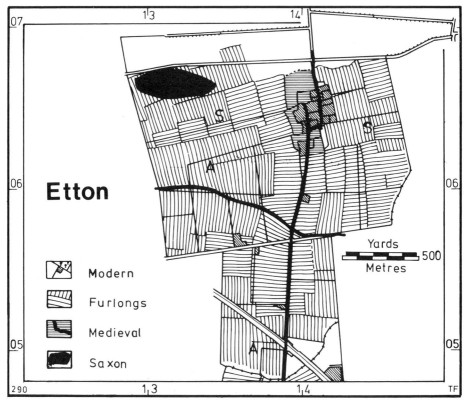

5
The origins of open fields

It is impossible to give a simple authoritative account for the origin of subdivided fields. They are so ancient that they long predate any detailed historical description. We can do no more than put together the fragmentary pieces of archaeological and historical evidence and conjecture. It is a topic that has received much attention for a century, and the suggestions and theories previously put forward must first be considered.

Theoretical and historical approaches

Seebohm, in 1883, put forward the idea that the three-field system went back to the early Saxon period and that much may have been inherited from the Roman or earlier periods. He ascribed the division of land into strips as the result of common ploughing, i.e. the plough team was shared and individual landholders contributed an ox or part of the plough. Every day one strip was ploughed and assigned to each contributor in turn.

In 1892 Vinogradoff suggested that strips resulted from an equal sharing of all types of land, good and bad, by the whole community; he was never explicit as to when he thought they were introduced. He did, however, consider them as part and parcel of a tribal communal holding of the land by a primitive agricultural society.

The two previous writers distinguished between Celtic systems and the two- or three-field system which was assumed to apply to all of England. In 1915 Gray published his detailed analysis of English field systems, classifying them into six types, and showed that they were quite complex.

The most extensive type was still the two- or three-field system which he called 'Midland'. On the western fringe he observed there were parishes with irregular fields, i.e. where there were more than three cropping assemblages of furlongs, or where there had been partial enclosure or the addition of assarted land. In East Anglia the strips of a holding were not spread uniformly throughout the township, there was more than one cropping arrangement and each manor within a village tended to retain rights over a particular part. In Kent holdings were also rather localised and not distributed: ownership, moreover, descended by equal shares (i.e. subdivisions) between heirs. The Lower Thames Basin was another region of iregularly arranged fields. Gray's sixth type was the Celtic system, of which the main characteristics were its smallness and the presence of infield and outfield cultivation (see above).

As regards the origin of open fields, he equated the Midland system with a region of intensive Saxon settlement and concluded therefore that it was brought over by Germanic settlers in the fifth century AD. He saw three-field systems as being a modification of two-field arrangements that had begun to occur in the thirteenth century.

The Orwins, in 1938, looked at the problem from the practical point of view. They considered that the use of a plough with a fixed mouldboard necessitated the ploughing of a strip and ridging it up in order to complete a day's work. To reduce the amount of turning with a long plough team, the shape of a plot would preferably be long in proportion to its width. The Orwins assumed that the Midland system had developed from a shifting arable system like the Scottish outfields.

Bishop (1935) and Homans (1941) saw assarting as being a prime cause for subdivision of holdings. As a new intake of land was cultivated it would be divided in proportion to how much land each person in the village owned. A growth of furlongs out from the village centre was envisaged.

In 1964 Thirsk defined a common field system as having four elements: subdivided fields, rights of common grazing or fallow, a common waste, and a village assembly for control of the whole system (manorial court). She argued that such systems could not suddenly appear and must have evolved. Furthermore, systems apparently similar at a late date may have arrived at that state by different means and at different times. It was considered that piecemeal colonisation of land and partible inheritance would cause a system of intermixed strips, and eventually it would be necessary to have some form of communal regulation of cropping. Thus it was an agricultural necessity and not an ancient tribal common ownership that created the Midland system. A date in the twelfth or thirteenth century was suggested for the completed mature two- and three-field systems.

A major study of regional types of field system was edited by Baker and Butlin in 1973, giving more detail than Gray and defining the problem to be solved more exactly. Many more inequalitites were discovered, even in the Midlands. Particular area studies showed conclusively that both piecemeal colonisation and partible inheritance were effective causes for the creation of subdivided fields. They thought that the trend would have been from disorder to order, i.e. irregular fields leading to regular ones, and that probably at one time most regions had a primitive infield-outfield system that developed into the others. Population growth was seen as the cause of pressure on land and it was supposed that the more organised Midland system came into operation in the early medieval period.

Two volumes deal specifically with the origins of field systems. Dodgshon (1980) does not see subdivided fields as the product of a tribally constituted farming community, but as the result of piecemeal colonisation. Neither does he agree that infield-outfield is an early prototype since there is no reference to it before the fourteenth century. It is merely a later development in parishes with a large available area of waste; the conditions of tenure show this: infield was ancient land assessed in bovates, virgates, etc, whereas outfield was free and held for a cash rent. A most important observation is that two- and three-field townships were formed as a result of the splitting up of larger estates. There is plenty of evidence to show that, in late Saxon times, estates often consisted of several settlements, which were later split up (see for instance the Berkshire Saxon charters). Such processes frequently meant that multiple estates, formerly including arable and waste, could be broken into new smaller lordships, some of which were detached from the waste. This would lead to the immediate necessity for fallow grazing and give the community the obvious opportunity to change the distribution of arable holdings into any convenient form that suited them at the time.

A report of a conference on the origins of open fields, edited by Rowley (1981), contains several important papers, including one by Fox, who demonstrated that the two- and three-field system was not an innovation of the twelfth century, being already well established. He also gives examples of the remodelling of the fields of some townships.

It is clear from the above that there have been many ideas put forward, some of them conflicting, to explain subdivided fields. The physical evidence can contribute two further pieces of information, one regarding Saxon settlements and the other showing major changes in furlong patterns.

The physical evidence

The evidence of archaeology has shown that the early theories of complete systems of Midland-type fields being brought to England by the early Saxon settlers, or continuing from the Roman period, cannot be correct. Aerial photography and excavation prove that strip fields are later than all Roman (and earlier) sites. More surprisingly, strips overlie early and middle Saxon sites as well (fig. 26). The early Saxon settlement pattern is not at all like that of the medieval nucleated village. Sites are limited to light soils, which suggests a primitive agriculture incapable of dealing with heavy clay land. The settlements are small and, where they occur, numerous, having a distribution like that of Roman and prehistoric sites. There is no evidence of subdivided fields associated with them. Therefore the theories of the early workers can be disregarded in so far as they claim that strip fields were introduced in the fifth century.

Archaeology can only give a rough guide to the date of strip fields. The strips must be later than the early Saxon sites, but the dating of these gives problems. The evidence of pottery shows that they were deserted before the middle of the ninth century, but how much before is difficult to say without excavation. However, what was happening to the settlement is of interest: it seems that the desertions were the result of deliberate replanning to form the present nucleated Midland village arrangement. Thus there are two 'catastrophic' events happening in the middle Saxon period: a resiting of villages, and the laying out of subdivided fields. If it be accepted that these events occurred together, then we have a dating for subdivided fields before the mid ninth century, perhaps in the eighth century.

The evidence of Saxon charters shows that open-field terminology is in use by the tenth century, and charters of 962 and *c* 977 for Hendred and Kingston, Oxfordshire, show unequivocally that a mixed strip system was in operation because the lands granted lay intermixed 'acre under acre'.

Changes in furlong patterns give some evidence of how the early strip fields were laid out, which has to be accounted for in an overall interpretation. As already stated, furlong patterns surveyed on the ground, or visible on air photographs, invariably correspond to open-field estate maps, showing that no major changes have occurred since the sixteenth century.

The late medieval reversion of arable areas to pasture allows us to view furlong patterns unchanged since the fourteenth and fifteenth centuries. In these ancient permanent pasture areas the patterns do not differ from those of the later arable, therefore any changes in furlong layout must date back well into the medieval period if not before. The case of Kislingbury supports such a contention because the seventeenth-century furlongs can be traced back to the early twelfth century.

The final layout for a given parish is principally dependent upon the landscape; since strips are generally aligned down the steepest gradient, there will be a larger number of small furlongs orientated in all directions in a region where an undulating landscape is dissected by a multiplicity of springs and brooks. On plains and terraces, as at Maxey and Etton in Cambridgeshire, furlong patterns are simple rectangular systems (fig. 26). This rectangularity seems to be the objec-

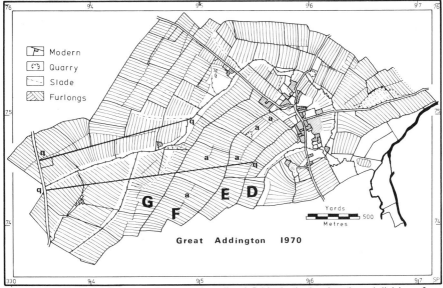

Fig. 27. Great Addington enclosure and medieval fields, both showing the subdivision of larger units (SP 9574).

tive of a mature open-field network.

Bishop and Homans suggested that open-field patterns are arrived at by a piecemeal reclamation of waste, perhaps taking in a furlong at a time, getting progressively further away from the village as the population grew. Many furlong patterns do show evidence of being based on the present villages, but there are puzzling aspects in the field patterns of the 120 Northamptonshire parishes that have been studied. How could tiny furlongs (marked 'S' on figs. 17 and 26) result from the reclamation of a block of land? Surely they are the result of subsequent changes. Most curious of all is the way in which some furlong boundaries suddenly cease so that two furlongs merge into one (marked 'A' on figs. 17 and 26).

Furlong patterns fit into the class of fields described by Bradley (in a prehistoric context) as cohesive. He showed that there were two essentially different types of field system, those formed by a process of accretion (i.e. piecemeal reclamation and addition of an irregular area to an existing field system) and those formed by subdivision of larger areas. The latter tend to be rectangular, or at least contain many long lines. In spite of all the irregularities imposed by the landscape, medieval fields fall clearly into the latter group.

The modern and medieval fields of Great Addington demonstrate this subdivision (fig. 27). Long lines of the eighteenth-century hedges to the west (qq) show that the enclosure was concerned with large blocks of land which were later divided into plots of about 10 hectares (25 acres). Similarly medieval furlongs E and F contain smaller subdivisions (aa) within their long lines. Furlongs D, E, F and G are themselves probably all subdivisions of a large block of land lying between two brooks.

Can any evidence be discovered to suggest that these modifications occurred? Wollaston demonstrates that some of the 'present' furlongs have been created by the division of furlongs with much longer strips. Fig. 28 compares a 1774 open-field map and an aerial photograph of 1948. The furlongs lie parallel to each other in several modern fields each with a different history of cultivation, from grass, undisturbed ridge and furrow, to fields ploughed once and fields ploughed many times. Those with undisturbed strips show the reversed S curve at the boundaries, but where modern destructive ploughing has begun the ancient furrows are seen to continue in a straight line under the boundary (fig. 28b, furlongs A and B). The only explanation is that the two furlongs were made out of one that originally had much longer strips, by cutting across all the strips and forming a new turning place. The shorter lands gradually developed reversed S profiles and piled-up banks of soil on the new boundary. North of the present road (which follows an ancient track called Thatchway) there are three furlongs with well developed reversed S lands at the boundaries. Not many of the furrows can be seen to continue under the boundaries, but there is an irregular sequence of narrow and wide lands visible on the original photograph, showing some similarity in all three furlongs. Although not exactly the same in sequence, there is much more correspondence than can be accidental, so providing further evidence of large-scale division.

Even better evidence can be found where furlongs were laid out on a long curve. At Raunds six furlongs in North Dale Field, with strips orientated in the same direction, make up one massive furlong with lands 1,000 metres (1,100 yards) long, lying in a smooth curve (apart from the reverse S at each of the boundaries). It is not possible for this to occur by piecemeal reclamation of waste, furlong by furlong; only a later subdivision would account for such an arrangement (fig. 29).

At Wadenhoe two furlongs lying either side of a road that has medieval origins have a curvature that shows they once formed a single large block (fig. 30).

Other examples of long 'ploughing curves' are preserved in the landscape, for example at Middleton, west of Pickering, North Yorkshire. Here the whole parish seems to have been laid out in two massive blocks with curved strips, preserved in the modern hedge

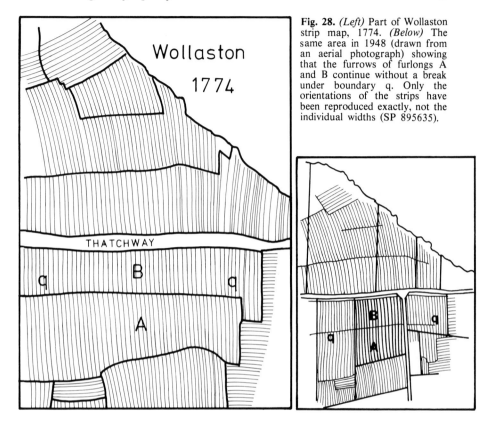

Fig. 28. *(Left)* Part of Wollaston strip map, 1774. *(Below)* The same area in 1948 (drawn from an aerial photograph) showing that the furrows of furlongs A and B continue without a break under boundary q. Only the orientations of the strips have been reproduced exactly, not the individual widths (SP 895635).

Wollaston
1774

THATCHWAY

q
B
q
A

lines, up to 2,000 metres (2,200 yards) long (fig. 31). It is not known whether there are any later subdivisions within these long curves.

On the Yorkshire Wolds the general layout of the landscape is in massive furlongs that run over the plateau from dale to dale, with strips up to 1,000 metres (1,100 yards) long (fig. 32). Similar long strips occur at Holderness.

In the silt fens of Lincolnshire, Norfolk and Cambridgeshire, the landscape is divided into long plots lying in parallel blocks. The strips are not ridged up and are separated by drainage ditches; they are frequently up to 1,200 metres (1,300 yards) in length (fig. 33).

It is clear, therefore, that on the periphery of the Midland region there are many surviving examples of landscapes laid out in massive blocks with long strips. The evidence given above suggests that some, at least, of the Midland area was also once so arranged.

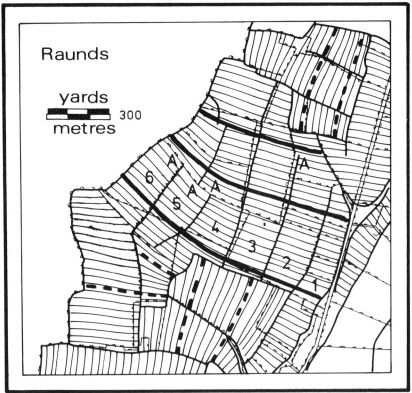

Fig. 29. Raunds, showing six furlongs created by subdividing a large area of strips which form a continuous smooth curve (TL 0074).

Fig. 30. A medieval road splitting a large curved furlong into two smaller parts, Wadenhoe (TL 005841).

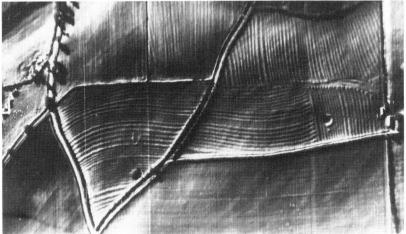

Historical data can be found to support the physical evidence. Detailed examination of field books for two Northamptonshire townships, Hardingstone and Muscott, dated respectively *c* 1660 and 1433, reveals some unexpected archaic features. Both field books have hidden in them a regular cycle of tenurial holdings that predate the furlongs being described. It is likely that both of these cycles are, at the latest, thirteenth-century in date. When the cycles are plotted on reconstructed furlong maps some remarkable features are discovered. Some of the furlong boundaries start or begin at the cycles,

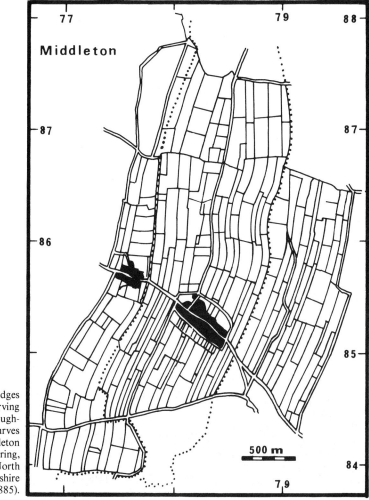

Fig. 31. Hedges preserving long ploughing curves at Middleton near Pickering, North Yorkshire (SE 7885).

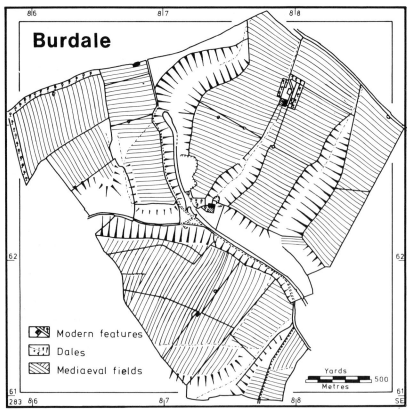

Fig. 32. Burdale, North Yorkshire, showing the field system consisting of long strips running from dale to dale. No attempt has been made to reproduce the exact number of strips; they are about 9 metres (10 yards) wide on the average (SE 8762).

and cycles often coincide in adjacent furlongs (fig. 34 qq). In other words the cycles are older than the furlong pattern and demonstrate an original layout on a large scale with long lands. Even more remarkably, in some of the smaller furlongs that interrupt this long furlong pattern, it is found that the number of lands is a multiple of the cycle. The Hardingstone cycle is thirty-two and furlongs going in the 'wrong' direction have thirty-two and sixty-four etc lands in them (fig. 34). This is explicable if it be assumed that the smaller 'cross furlongs' have been deliberately changed because of some local drainage requirement. Doing this in a whole number of cycles would ensure that everyone had the same amount of land after the changeover, and it could be done piecemeal, without a reordering of strips in the whole township. So at Hardingstone and Muscott there is historical evidence for Midland townships being originally laid out on the large scale; subsequent piecemeal changes, demanded by the lie of the land, account for the final complex pattern. The process of subdivision is envisaged as occurring before the thirteenth century, probably appreciably before.

The two pieces of physical evidence suggest that for Northamptonshire, at least, strip fields have a middle Saxon origin, and that some strips were laid out on the large scale — a strip system from the beginning. This latter point would seem to disagree with models of cultivated fields arising as a result of piecemeal colonisation. In the case of the early Saxon settlement areas, i.e. the rich loams of river gravels, piecemeal colonisation would not be expected, because the early settlers found an organised and cultivated Roman landscape. They merely took it over and in many cases continued to live on villa sites for a time. On the other hand, where heavy clay soils were not settled until much later the countryside would rapidly revert to a wild state, and piecemeal reclamation would probably be necessary at a later date when settlements and fields expanded.

The very long strips set out originally would seem to support the Orwins' idea that the fixed mouldboard technology necessitated long

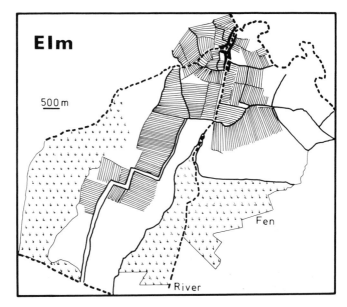

Fig. 33. Elm, Cambridgeshire, showing a ditched field system consisting of blocks of strips up to 1,200 metres (1,300 yards) long (TF 4604).

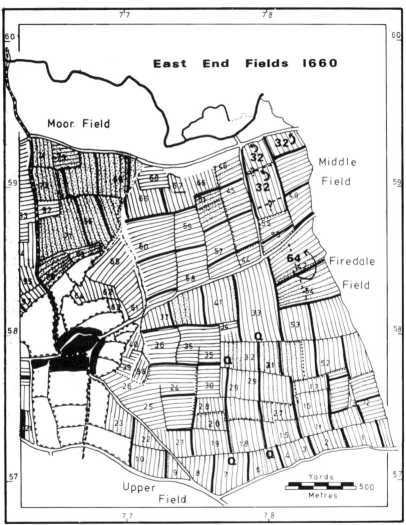

Fig. 34. Hardingstone, showing regular cycles of tenurial holdings (thirteenth century) that predate some of the furlong boundaries (SP 7758).

furrows; there was clearly no desire to create more rectangular plots even though the original holding could be over a hectare ($2\frac{1}{2}$ acres) in size.

The large-scale planning and later subdivision to form furlongs explain why there are so few Latin or Celtic elements in medieval topographical names — there just is no continuity, and generally furlong boundaries have not the slightest relation to earlier landscape features.

The continental European evidence also shows that a large-scale planned layout of field systems is quite normal. In southern Germany and Austria many parishes survived intact with strips running from the village to the parish boundary. The German examples have been conclusively dated to settlement associated with the eastern expansion of the Carolingian Empire during the period 775-850.

The factors causing the establishment of strip fields are thus seen to be complex: in different regions some forces would be more dominant than others, hence the great variety in types of field system. The main factors seem to be the desire for equal sharing, piecemeal reclamation and possibly the splitting up of holdings between heirs. Later in- fluences such as population pressure and sudden loss of pasture by township splitting would lead to an organised two- or three-field system by remodelling. A monocausal explanation is not possible to account for all the complex types of field system found in Great Britain.

6
Bibliography

Ault, W. O. *Open Field Farming in Medieval England*. 1969.

Baker, A. R. H. and Butlin, R. A. (editors). *Field Systems of the British Isles*. 1973.

Beresford, M. W. *History on the Ground*. Second edition, 1971.

Beresford, M. W. and St Joseph, J. K. S. *Medieval England — an Aerial Survey*. Second edition 1979.

Biddick, K. (editor). *Proceedings of Fifteenth International Congress for Medieval Studies at Western Michigan University*. 1982.

Dodgshon, R. A. *The Origins of British Field Systems, An Interpretation*. 1980.

Gelling, M. *The Place-Names of Berkshire*. Volume III, 1976.

Gray, H. L. *English Field Systems*. 1915.

Hall, C. P. and Ravensdale, J. R. *The West Fields of Cambridge*. 1976.

Hall, D. N. 'Hardingstone parish survey'. *Northants Archaeology* 15 (1980) 119-32.

Orwin, C. S. and C. S. *The Open Fields*. Third edition, 1967.

Rowley, R. T. (editor). *The Origin of Open Fields*. 1981.

West, J. *Village Records*. 1962.

Index